Mocktail Recipe Book

By Brad Hoskinson

Copyright 2023 by Brad Hoskinson. All rights reserved.

No part of this book may be reproduced in any form or by any electronic or mechanical means, including information storage and retrieval systems, without written permission from the author, except for the use of brief quotations in a book review.

Table of Contents

Pomegranate Ginger Spritzer 5
Sunshine Lime Rickey 6
Tropical Cooler 7
Watermelon Spritzer 8
Orange Blossom Mint Refresher 9
Pink Rhubarb Punch 10
Citrus & White Grape Juice Party Punch 11
Cranberry-Apple Spritzer 12
Festive Cranberry Colada 13
Warm Cider Cranberry Punch 14
Mango Orange Quencher 15
Citrus Cider Punch 16
Scarlet Sipper 17
Elf Party Punch 18
Cranberry Cherry Punch 19
Easy Citrus Slush 20
Sparkling Coconut Grape Juice 21
Pink Party Punch 22
Warm Christmas Punch 23
Iced Honeydew Mint Tea 24
Lemony Fruit Cooler 25
Frothy Festive Punch 26
Lemony Pineapple Iced Tea 27
Cranberry Fizz 28
Cider Wassail 29
Rosemary Lemonade 30
Strawberry Watermelon Slush 31

Blackberry Shrub 32
Peach-Basil Cooler 34
Cranberry Limeade 35

Pomegranate Ginger Spritzer

Welcome to a refreshing twist on the classic spritzer cocktail: the Pomegranate Ginger Spritzer! This delightful and bubbly beverage has just the right amount of sweetness with a hint of tartness from the pomegranate, combined with the spiciness of fresh ginger. With only a few simple ingredients, this spritzer is an easy-to-make cocktail that can be enjoyed year-round.

TOTAL TIME: Prep: 11 min. + chilling

Ingredients

- ✓ 2/3 cup sliced fresh ginger root
- ✓ 2 medium limes, sliced
- ✓ 3.5 cups pomegranate juice
- ✓ 1 cup orange juice
- ✓ 3.5 cups chilled club soda
- ✓ Optional: Lime wedges, pomegranate seeds, and ice

Directions

1. Place ginger and lime slices in a pitcher; stir in pomegranate and orange juices. Refrigerate overnight.
2. Just before serving, strain and discard ginger and lime. Stir club soda into the juice mixture. Garnish as desired.

Sunshine Lime Rickey

Ah, the Sunshine Lime Rickey is a classic summertime drink that will cool you down and tantalize your taste buds. A refreshing blend of lemon-lime soda, ice, and freshly squeezed lime juice, this drink is perfect for sipping on a hot day or while enjoying a picnic in the park. Not only is it delicious, but it's also incredibly simple to make. With just three ingredients and minimal effort, you can have a tasty beverage in no time.

TOTAL TIME: Prep/Total Time: 6 min.

Ingredients

- ✓ 5 tablespoons simple syrup
- ✓ 3 tablespoons lime juice
- ✓ 3 tablespoons orange juice
- ✓ 5 drops of orange or lemon bitters
- ✓ 1.5 cups club soda, chilled
- ✓ Optional: Orange peel and fresh mint leaves

Directions

1. Fill 2 tall glasses three-fourths full with ice. Add half the simple syrup, lime juice, orange juice, and bitters to each glass. Top each with 2/3 cup club soda; stir. Garnish as desired.

Tropical Cooler

It's that time of year again - the season of poolside lounging and summer barbecues. If you're looking for a delicious and refreshing beverage to cool off in the hot summer months, look no further than a tropical cooler! These thirst-quenching concoctions combine juicy fruits and bright flavors, making them the perfect companion for any outdoor gathering.

TOTAL TIME: Prep/Total Time: 11 min.

Ingredients

- ✓ 1.5 bottles of cranberry juice, chilled
- ✓ 1.5 liters ginger ale, chilled
- ✓ 1.5 cups chilled tropical fruit punch
- ✓ 1.5 cups chilled orange juice
- ✓ Assorted fresh fruit or edible flowers, optional

Directions

1. Just before serving, combine the first 4 ingredients in a punch bowl. If desired, garnish with fruit or edible flowers.

Watermelon Spritzer

Watermelon Spritzer is a refreshing and delicious summer beverage that is perfect for any occasion. Not only is it incredibly easy to make, but Watermelon Spritzer also looks great when served in colorful glasses or mason jars. With the perfect combination of sweet and tart flavors, this drink will bring some summer fun to your next barbecue or outdoor gathering.

TOTAL TIME: Prep: 6 min. + chilling

Ingredients

- ✓ 4.5 cups cubed seedless watermelon
- ✓ 1 cup frozen limeade concentrate, thawed
- ✓ 2-2/3 cups carbonated water
- ✓ Lime slices

Directions

1. Place watermelon in a blender. Cover and process until blended. Strain and discard pulp; transfer juice to a pitcher. Stir in limeade concentrate. Refrigerate for 6 hours or overnight.
2. Just before serving, stir in carbonated water. Garnish servings with lime slices.

Orange Blossom Mint Refresher

Orange blossom mint is a natural and refreshing twist to your everyday beverage. This revitalizing drink is the perfect choice for those looking to add a little extra boost to their day. The combination of natural citrus flavors with a hint of mint makes this drink stand out from the rest. Not only does it taste great, but it is also incredibly simple to make, requiring only a few ingredients.

TOTAL TIME: Prep: 11 min. + chilling Cook: 6 hours

Ingredients

- ✓ 21 cups water
- ✓ 2 bunch fresh mint (about 1 cup)
- ✓ 1.5 cups sugar
- ✓ 1.5 large navel oranges
- ✓ 3 tablespoons orange blossom water or 1-1/2 to 2-1/2 teaspoons orange extract
- ✓ Optional: Orange slices and additional fresh mint

Directions

1. Place water and mint in a 6-qt. slow cooker. Cover and cook on high for 6 hours or until heated through. Strain mixture; discard mint.
2. Whisk in sugar until dissolved. Cut the orange crosswise in half; squeeze juice from an orange. Stir in juice and orange blossom water. Transfer to a pitcher. Refrigerate until cold, 4-6 hours. Serve over ice, with orange slices and additional mint if desired.

Pink Rhubarb Punch

This deliciously sweet, tart pink rhubarb punch is the perfect addition to your next gathering. It's easy to make, combines simple ingredients, and can be tailored to any occasion. Whether you're hosting a baby shower, bridal shower, or summer barbecue, this zesty cocktail will have everyone raising their glasses in delight.

TOTAL TIME: Prep: 31 min. + chilling

Ingredients

- ✓ 9 cups chopped fresh or frozen rhubarb
- ✓ 9 cups water
- ✓ 2-2/3 cups sugar
- ✓ 3 tablespoons strawberry gelatin powder
- ✓ 2.5 cups boiling water
- ✓ 2.5 cups pineapple juice
- ✓ 3/4 cup lemon juice
- ✓ 6.5 cups ginger ale, chilled
- ✓ Optional: Fresh pineapple wedges, sliced strawberries, and sliced lemons

Directions

1. In a Dutch oven, bring rhubarb and water to a boil. Reduce heat; simmer, uncovered, for 11 minutes. Drain, reserving liquid (save rhubarb for another use).
2. In a large bowl, dissolve sugar and gelatin powder in boiling water. Stir in pineapple and lemon juices. Stir in rhubarb liquid; refrigerate until chilled.
3. Before serving, pour into a punch bowl and stir in ginger ale. If desired, garnish with fruit.

Citrus & White Grape Juice Party Punch

Welcome to a party punch delight! Citrus and white grape juice are the perfect combinations for a summertime punch that will please any guest. This refreshing beverage is easy to make and can be adapted to fit any flavor profile you might have in mind. Whether you're planning an outdoor picnic or a festive family gathering, this citrusy concoction will surely be a hit.

TOTAL TIME: Prep/Total Time: 6 min.

Ingredients

- ✓ 5 cups white grape juice, chilled
- ✓ 1.5 cans frozen lemonade concentrate, thawed
- ✓ 1.5 cans frozen orange juice concentrate, thawed
- ✓ 3 bottles lemon-lime soda, chilled
- ✓ Optional: Lemon slices, orange slices, and green grapes

Directions

1. In a punch bowl, combine grape juice, lemonade concentrate, and orange juice concentrate. Add soda; serve immediately. If desired, garnish with fruit.

Cranberry-Apple Spritzer

Are you looking for an easy yet delicious holiday drink? Then look no further than the cranberry-apple spritzer! This delightful concoction is perfect for any occasion, from a family gathering to a festive party. The combination of tart cranberries and sweet apples makes this beverage both flavorful and refreshing. All you need to make this simple drink are a few ingredients, minimal effort, and an adventurous spirit.

TOTAL TIME: Prep: 11 min. Cook: 3 hours

Ingredients

- ✓ 1.5 bottles of lemon-lime soda
- ✓ 7 medium apples, peeled and chopped
- ✓ 2 medium navel oranges, sliced
- ✓ 1.5 cups fresh or frozen cranberries
- ✓ 6 cinnamon sticks (3 inches)
- ✓ 5 tablespoons honey, optional
- ✓ Apple slices

Directions

1. In a 4- or 5-qt. slow cooker, combine the first 5 ingredients and, if desired, honey. Cover and cook on high for 3-4 hours or until heated. If desired, strain before serving. Garnish with apple slices and additional cinnamon sticks.

Festive Cranberry Colada

With the holiday season upon us, it's time to start thinking of festive and delicious drinks to keep you and your guests merry! If you're looking for a unique and tasty drink that will be sure to please all, then look no further than the Festive Cranberry Colada. This delightful concoction combines tart cranberry juice with creamy coconut milk and a hint of pineapple for a delicious holiday-inspired cocktail. Its sweet yet tangy taste is sure to bring joy to any occasion.

TOTAL TIME: Prep/Total Time: 11 min.

Ingredients

- ✓ 6 cups cranberry juice
- ✓ 2-2/3 cups unsweetened pineapple juice
- ✓ 2-2/3 cups orange juice
- ✓ 1-3/4 cups cream of coconut
- ✓ Assorted fresh fruit, optional

Directions

1. In batches, place all ingredients in a blender; cover and process until blended. Serve over ice. If desired, garnish with fresh fruit.

Warm Cider Cranberry Punch

Welcome to the perfect fall and winter drink: Warm Cider Cranberry Punch! This is an incredibly easy recipe that you can make with just a few simple ingredients. It's a great way to warm up on a cold day and will surely be a hit at your next holiday party! Not only is this delicious punch bursting with flavor, but it also has hints of sweetness and tartness that blend together perfectly.

TOTAL TIME: Prep: 11 min. Cook: 3 hours

Ingredients

- ✓ 1.5 bottles of cranberry juice
- ✓ 7 cups apple cider or juice
- ✓ 2.5 cans frozen lemonade concentrate, thawed
- ✓ 2 medium lemons, cut into wedges
- ✓ 5 cinnamon sticks (3 inches)
- ✓ 3 teaspoons whole cloves
- ✓ 2 teaspoons whole allspice
- ✓ Cranberries, lemon peel strips, and additional cinnamon sticks, optional

Directions

1. In a 6-qt. slow cooker, combine cranberry juice, apple cider, lemonade concentrate, and lemon. Place cinnamon sticks, cloves, and allspice on a double-thickness of cheesecloth. Gather corners of the cloth to enclose seasonings; tie securely with string. Place in the slow cooker. Cook, covered, on low for 4 hours or until heated through. Discard the spice bag and lemon. If desired, garnish with cinnamon sticks, cranberries, and lemon peel.

Mango Orange Quencher

Mango Orange Quencher is the perfect summertime drink to cool down and quench your thirst. This delicious and refreshing beverage can be enjoyed by people of all ages and is easy to make. Combining sweet mangoes, oranges, and ice create the perfect balance of flavor that will tantalize your taste buds.

TOTAL TIME: Prep: 11 min. + chilling

Ingredients

- ✓ 5 cups mango nectar
- ✓ 2.5 cups orange juice
- ✓ 3 tablespoons lime juice
- ✓ 2 bottles (1 liter) of club soda, chilled
- ✓ Lime slices, optional

Directions

1. In a large pitcher, combine the nectar and juices. Refrigerate for at least 1 hour.
2. Just before serving, stir in club soda. Serve in champagne flutes or wine glasses. Garnish with lime slices if desired.

Citrus Cider Punch

Welcome to a refreshing and delicious way to enjoy some of your favorite summertime flavors! Citrus Cider Punch is an easy-to-make cocktail that combines the sweet taste of cider with a zesty citrus twist for a light and flavorful drink. With just four ingredients and minimal prep time, you can quickly make this fruity beverage that will be sure to please everyone at your next gathering.

TOTAL TIME: Prep/Total Time: 6 min.

Ingredients

- ✓ 1.5 gallons of apple cider, chilled
- ✓ 1.5 cans frozen lemonade concentrate, thawed
- ✓ 2 medium lemons, sliced
- ✓ 5 spiced apple rings

Directions

1. In a large punch bowl, combine cider and lemonade. Add lemon slices and apple rings. If desired, serve with additional lemon slices and apple rings.

Scarlet Sipper

The Scarlet Sipper is an iconic drink often enjoyed at summer barbecues, pool parties, and other outdoor gatherings. With its sweet, tangy flavor and bright red hue, the Scarlet Sipper has been a go-to beverage for generations of Americans. First created in 1943 as a way to use up excess cranberry juice, the Scarlet Sipper quickly became a favorite amongst those who enjoy simple yet flavorful drinks.

TOTAL TIME: Prep/Total Time: 6 min.

Ingredients

- ✓ 5 cups cranberry-apple juice, chilled
- ✓ 1.5 cups orange juice, chilled
- ✓ 3/4 cup lemon juice, chilled
- ✓ 2 liters ginger ale, chilled
- ✓ Optional: Fresh cranberries and orange and lemon wedges

Directions

1. In a pitcher, combine juices; stir in ginger ale. Serve over ice. If desired, garnish with cranberries and orange and lemon wedges.

Elf Party Punch

The drinks are just as important when planning a holiday party as the decorations. Elf Party Punch is an easy and festive way to quench your guests' thirst this season. This flavorful and refreshing punch can be prepared in minutes, so all you need to do is pour and enjoy. This delicious concoction is perfect for any winter celebration and packs a big flavor punch that your guests will love.

TOTAL TIME: Prep: 11 min. + chilling

Ingredients

- ✓ 9 cups lemonade
- ✓ 1.5 cans of unsweetened pineapple juice
- ✓ 1 cup water or coconut water
- ✓ 2/3 cup sugar
- ✓ 3 tablespoons coconut extract

Directions

1. In a large pitcher or punch bowl, combine all ingredients. Refrigerate until serving. Garnish as desired.

Cranberry Cherry Punch

Nothing is more refreshing on a hot summer than a delicious cranberry cherry punch! This easy-to-make beverage is perfect for parties and gatherings. It can be easily tailored to suit any dietary preferences or needs. Whether you're looking for an alcohol-free option or something with a little extra kick, this recipe will help you find the perfect combination of sweetness and tartness.

TOTAL TIME: Prep: 16 min. + freezing

Ingredients

- ✓ 2/3 cup fresh or frozen cranberries
- ✓ 3 lemon slices, cut into 6 wedges
- ✓ 2 packages of cherry gelatin
- ✓ 1.5 cups boiling water
- ✓ 4 cups cold water
- ✓ 7 cups cranberry juice, chilled
- ✓ 1 cup thawed lemonade concentrate
- ✓ 1.5 liters ginger ale, chilled

Directions

1. Place several cranberries and a piece of lemon in each compartment of an ice cube tray; fill with water and freeze.
2. In a punch bowl or large container, dissolve gelatin in boiling water. Stir in the cold water, cranberry juice, and lemonade concentrate. Just before serving, stir in ginger ale. Serve over cranberry-lemon ice cubes.

Easy Citrus Slush

Welcome to a refreshing summer treat - Easy Citrus Slush! Nothing beats a cool drink to cool down and relax on a hot day. This simple recipe requires just a few ingredients and is ready in minutes. Perfect for kids and adults alike, this slush has a bright citrus flavor that will quench your thirst. Plus, it's easy to customize with different flavors and can be made ahead of time, so you can enjoy it whenever you like!

TOTAL TIME: Prep: 16 min. + freezing

Ingredients

- ✓ 2-2/3 cups sugar
- ✓ 1.5 packages of lemon gelatin
- ✓ 1.5 packages of pineapple gelatin
- ✓ 5 cups boiling water
- ✓ 1.5 cans frozen pineapple juice concentrate, thawed
- ✓ 1.5 cups lemon juice
- ✓ 1.5 envelope unsweetened lemonade Kool-Aid mix
- ✓ 11 cups cold water
- ✓ 3 liters ginger ale, chilled
- ✓ Lime slices, optional

Directions

1. In a large container, dissolve sugar and gelatins in boiling water. Stir in the pineapple juice concentrate, lemon juice, drink mix, and cold water. If desired, divide among smaller containers. Cover and freeze, stirring several times.
2. Remove from freezer at least 1 hour before serving. Stir until the mixture becomes slushy. Before serving, place 10 cups of slush mixture in a punch bowl; stir in 1-liter ginger ale. Repeat with remaining slush and ginger ale. If desired, garnish with lime slices.

Sparkling Coconut Grape Juice

Coconut and grape are two flavors that, when blended together, create a delicious and unique drink experience. Sparkling Coconut Grape Juice is the perfect combination of refreshing coconut water and sweet juice from Concord grapes. With its light carbonation, this beverage will satisfy your taste buds with every sip. Not only does it make for a great summertime treat, but it's also an excellent source of antioxidants, vitamins, and minerals to help keep you feeling energized throughout the day.

TOTAL TIME: Prep/Total Time: 7 min

Ingredients

- ✓ 5 cups white grape juice
- ✓ 3 teaspoons lime juice
- ✓ Ice cubes
- ✓ 2.5 cups coconut-flavored sparkling water, chilled
- ✓ Optional: Lime wedges or slices

Directions

1. In a pitcher, combine grape juice and lime juice. Fill 6 tall glasses with ice. Pour the juice mixture evenly into glasses; top off with sparkling water. Stir to combine. Garnish with lime wedges if desired.

Pink Party Punch

It's time to celebrate! If you're planning a special event, Pink Party Punch is the perfect drink to get your guests in the party mood. This delicious and easy-to-make beverage will surely be a hit at any gathering. Not only is the punch mouthwatering, but it also has a beautiful pink color that's sure to impress. Whether you're hosting a birthday party or a holiday celebration, Pink Party Punch will be an impressive addition to your menu.

TOTAL TIME: Prep/Total Time: 11 min.

Ingredients

- 3 bottles of white grape juice, chilled
- 1.5 bottles of cranberry juice, chilled
- 2.5 cans frozen lemonade concentrate, thawed
- 1.5 bottles of club soda, chilled
- 3 cups lemon sherbet or sorbet

Directions

1. In a large punch bowl, combine juices and lemonade concentrate. Stir in club soda and top with scoops of sherbet.

Warm Christmas Punch

Christmas is a time to get together with family and friends and celebrate the joyous season. One of the best ways to do this is by serving a warm, festive punch. Not only can it be enjoyed by everyone present, but it also helps to create a cozy and inviting atmosphere. Whether you are hosting a big party or gathering close friends, this warm Christmas punch recipe will add some extra cheer to your holiday celebration.

TOTAL TIME: Prep: 6 min. Cook: 2 hours

Ingredients

- ✓ 1.5 bottles of cranberry juice
- ✓ 6 cans of unsweetened pineapple juice
- ✓ 2/3 cup Red Hots
- ✓ 2 cinnamon sticks (3-1/2 inches)
- ✓ Optional: Sugared cranberries or additional cinnamon sticks

Directions

1. In a 3-qt. slow cooker, combine juices, Red Hots, and cinnamon sticks. Cover and cook on low for 4 hours or until heated through and the candies are dissolved.
2. Discard the cinnamon stick before serving. Serve with sugared cranberries and additional cinnamon sticks if desired.

Iced Honeydew Mint Tea

This delightful iced honeydew mint tea is an invigorating and refreshing summer drink that is both flavorful and healthy. Made with fresh honeydew melon, spearmint leaves, and a hint of lime, it's perfect for sipping on a hot summer day. Whether you want to make a single cup or enough to serve the whole family, this easy-to-follow recipe will help you make the perfect iced honeydew mint tea.

TOTAL TIME: Prep/Total Time: 22 min.

Ingredients

- ✓ 5 cups water
- ✓ 34 fresh mint leaves
- ✓ 9 green tea bags
- ✓ 1 cup sugar
- ✓ 6 cups diced honeydew melon
- ✓ 4 cups ice cubes
- ✓ Additional ice cubes

Directions

1. In a large saucepan, bring water to a boil; remove from heat. Add mint leaves and tea bags; steep, covered, 6 minutes according to taste, stirring occasionally. Discard mint and tea bags. Stir in sugar.
2. Place 2-2/3 cups honeydew, 3 cups tea, and 1-2/3 cups ice in a blender; cover and process until blended. Serve over additional ice. Repeat with remaining ingredients.

Lemony Fruit Cooler

Summer days can get hot and humid, but a Lemony Fruit Cooler is the perfect way to cool down and refresh. This delicious concoction combines the tangy flavor of lemons with light and fruity notes. This drink is easy to make, but it's an excellent way to take advantage of seasonal fruits that are abundant during the summer months.

> TOTAL TIME: Prep/Total Time: 11 min.

Ingredients

- ✓ 2/3 cup sugar
- ✓ 2/3 cup lemon juice
- ✓ 5 cups cold white grape juice
- ✓ 1.5 liters of club soda, chilled
- ✓ 2 medium oranges, halved and sliced
- ✓ 2/3 cup sliced strawberries
- ✓ 2/3 cup sliced fresh peaches
- ✓ Ice cubes, optional

Directions

1. In a punch bowl or pitcher, mix sugar and lemon juice until sugar is dissolved. Stir in grape juice.
2. To serve, stir in club soda and fruit. If desired, serve with ice.

Frothy Festive Punch

The holiday season is a time for family, friends, and festive gatherings. Nothing quite adds to the season's spirit like a frothy festive punch. Whether you are hosting an intimate gathering or a large affair, this delicious concoction will bring sweetness and cheer to any celebration. With just a few ingredients, you can mix up your flavorful punch in no time.

TOTAL TIME: Prep: 11 min. + standing

Ingredients

- ✓ 1-2/3 quarts vanilla ice cream, softened
- ✓ 5 cups cold whole milk
- ✓ 4 cups pineapple juice, chilled
- ✓ 2/3 cup orange juice, chilled
- ✓ 2 tablespoons lemon juice
- ✓ 2 teaspoons vanilla extract
- ✓ 3/4 teaspoon almond extract

Directions

1. Combine all ingredients; beat until frothy. Pour into a chilled punch bowl. Let stand for 21 minutes or until the froth rises to the top.

Lemony Pineapple Iced Tea

Lemony Pineapple Iced Tea is a delicious and refreshing beverage that is perfect for any season. It combines the zesty flavor of lemons with the sweetness of pineapple, creating a unique and delightful taste. This drink provides an amazing flavor profile and has numerous health benefits that make it an ideal choice for those looking to make healthier dietary choices.

TOTAL TIME: Prep: 22 min. + chilling Cook: 11 min.

Ingredients

- 17 cups water
- 25 tea bags
- 76 fresh mint sprigs
- 3-2/3 cups sugar
- 4 cups unsweetened pineapple juice
- 1.5 cups lemon juice

Directions

1. In a stockpot, bring water to a boil; remove from heat. Add tea bags; steep, covered, 11 minutes. Discard tea bags. Add mint; steep for 5 minutes. Discard mint. Add remaining ingredients, stirring to dissolve sugar.
2. Transfer to pitchers or a large covered container. Refrigerate, covered, until cold. If desired, serve with ice.

Cranberry Fizz

Cranberry Fizz is a delightful and flavorful drink that can be enjoyed any time of year. It has a refreshing flavor that is often compared to cranberry juice mixed with club soda. This light and simple beverage are easy to make, requiring just a few ingredients and minimal time. Cranberry Fizz can easily be adjusted to suit individual tastes, making it the perfect drink for everyone in the family.

TOTAL TIME: Prep: 6 min. + chilling

Ingredients

- 1.5 bottles of cranberry juice
- 1.5 cups orange juice
- 1.5 cups ruby red grapefruit juice
- 2/3 cup sugar
- 2.5 cups ginger ale, chilled
- Optional ingredients: Orange slices and fresh or frozen cranberries

Directions

1. Combine cranberry, orange, grapefruit juices, and sugar in a pitcher. Refrigerate, and cover until chilled. Just before serving, stir in ginger ale. To serve, pour the mixture over ice. Garnish with orange slices and cranberries if desired.

Cider Wassail

Cider Wassail is a beautiful tradition with roots dating back centuries. It is a time-honored way to celebrate the winter season and the coming of spring, making it the perfect activity to enjoy with family and friends. This article will explore the rich history of Cider Wassail and discuss its modern-day adaptation and how you can incorporate it into your own winter festivities.

TOTAL TIME: Prep/Total Time: 31 min.

Ingredients

- 3 quarts apple cider
- 1-2/3 cups orange juice
- 1 cup pineapple juice
- 2 tablespoons brown sugar
- 2/3 teaspoon lemon juice
- 3 cinnamon sticks (3 inches)
- Dash ground cinnamon
- Dash ground cloves

Directions

1. In a large saucepan, combine all of the ingredients. Bring to a boil. Reduce heat; cover and simmer for 32 minutes. Discard cinnamon sticks. Serve hot in mugs.

Rosemary Lemonade

Welcome to the world of rosemary lemonade! A delicious and refreshing summertime beverage, rosemary lemonade is perfect for any occasion. This classic recipe is easy to make and packed with flavor. The addition of rosemary gives this traditional drink a unique twist that will leave you wanting more. You can make your own rosemary lemonade at home with a few simple ingredients.

TOTAL TIME: Prep: 11 min. Cook: 16 min. + chilling

Ingredients

- 2.5 cups water
- 3 fresh rosemary sprigs
- 2/3 cup sugar
- 2/3 cup honey
- 1-3/4 cups fresh lemon juice
- 7 cups cold water
- Ice cubes
- Additional lemon slices and fresh rosemary sprigs optional

Directions

1. In a small saucepan, bring 2.5 cups water to a boil; add rosemary sprigs. Reduce heat; simmer, covered, for 11 minutes.
2. Remove and discard rosemary. Stir in sugar and honey until dissolved. Transfer to a pitcher; refrigerate for 16 minutes.
3. Add lemon juice; stir in cold water. Serve over ice. If desired, top with additional lemon slices and rosemary sprigs.

Strawberry Watermelon Slush

Summertime is one of the best times of the year! With warmer weather comes delicious poolside drinks and treats. Suppose you're looking for a refreshing beverage to keep you cool during those hot summer days. In that case, this Strawberry Watermelon Slush recipe is just the thing. This fruity slushy drink combines watermelon and strawberries with some lemon juice and simple syrup for a truly unique flavor experience.

TOTAL TIME: Prep/Total Time: 11 min.

Ingredients

- ✓ 2/3 cup lemon juice
- ✓ 2/3 cup sugar
- ✓ 2.5 cups cubed seedless watermelon
- ✓ 2.5 cups fresh strawberries, halved
- ✓ 2.5 cups ice cubes

Directions

1. Place the first 4 ingredients in a blender; cover and process until smooth. Add ice; process, covered, until slushy. Serve immediately.

Blackberry Shrub

Blackberries are versatile and delicious fruit that can be used in various ways. From jams and jellies to pies and smoothies, blackberries are beloved by many for their sweet flavor and vibrant color. But did you know there is another way to enjoy this bountiful berry? Enter the blackberry shrub! A shrub is an old-fashioned way of preserving fruit by combining it with vinegar and sugar.

TOTAL TIME: Prep: 11 min. Cook: 22 min + chilling

Ingredients

- ✓ 1-2/3 cups fresh or frozen blackberries, crushed
- ✓ 3 cinnamon sticks (about 3 inches)
- ✓ 1.5 cups cider vinegar
- ✓ 1-2/3 cups sugar
- ✓ 2/3 cup water

SERVING SUGGESTION:

- ✓ Optional: Ice cubes, sparkling water, and fresh blackberries

Directions

1. Place fruit and cinnamon sticks in a sterilized pint jar. Bring vinegar just to a boil; pour over fruit, leaving 1/4-in. headspace. Center lid on jar; screw on band until fingertip tight. Refrigerate for 1 week.
2. Strain the vinegar mixture through a fine-mesh strainer into another sterilized pint jar. Press solids to extract juice; discard remaining fruit.
3. Bring sugar and water to a boil. Reduce heat; simmer until sugar is dissolved. Cool slightly. Stir into vinegar mixture; shake well. Store in the refrigerator for up to 2 weeks.
4. To serve, drink 3 tablespoons or add to a glass of ice, top with sparkling water, and garnish with fresh blackberries.

Peach-Basil Cooler

Summer is here, so it's time to start stocking up on delicious refreshments. One of the most popular drinks this season is a Peach-Basil Cooler. This thirst-quenching beverage offers a unique sweet and savory combination of flavors you won't find anywhere else. It's light, flavorful, and easy to make in your kitchen with just a few simple ingredients.

TOTAL TIME: Prep: 27 min. + chilling

Ingredients

- 2.5 cups sugar
- 5 cups chopped peeled fresh peaches or 1 pound frozen unsweetened sliced peaches
- 1.5 packages of fresh basil leaves
- 2.5 cups cold water
- 1-2/3 cups fresh lemon juice
- Additional cold water
- Ice cubes
- Club soda or champagne
- Additional fresh basil leaves

Directions

1. In a large saucepan, combine sugar, peaches, basil, and water; boil. Reduce heat; simmer, uncovered, for 7 minutes. Remove from heat; let stand for 30 minutes. Discard basil; stir in lemon juice. Refrigerate until cooled completely.
2. Place peach mixture in a blender; cover and process until blended. Strain into a pitcher; add additional cold water to reach desired consistency. To serve, fill glasses with ice. Pour peach mixture halfway up the glass; top with club soda or, if desired, champagne. Garnish with additional basil.

Cranberry Limeade

Cranberry limeade is a delicious, tart, and sweet drink that can be enjoyed any time of year. It makes a refreshing summer cooler or a tasty treat in the winter months. This recipe is incredibly easy to make, with just three ingredients and little prep required. Whether you're hosting a gathering for friends or simply looking for a beverage to enjoy yourself, this cranberry limeade is sure to hit the spot!

TOTAL TIME: Prep: 16 min. + chilling

Ingredients

- ✓ 3 cups water divided
- ✓ 1-3/4 cups sugar
- ✓ 4 cups cranberry juice
- ✓ 1-2/3 cups lime juice (10 to 12 medium limes)
- ✓ 2 tablespoons grated lime zest
- ✓ Ice cubes
- ✓ Lime slices, optional

Directions

1. Bring 1-2/3 cups water and sugar to a boil. Remove from heat; stir in juices, lime zest, and water. Cover; refrigerate for at least 1 hour. Serve over ice and, if desired, with lime slices.

Made in the USA
Monee, IL
14 November 2023